EMMANUEL JOSEPH

Action Speaks Louder, Leadership, Public Speaking, and the Art of Building Trust in Relationships

Copyright © 2025 by Emmanuel Joseph

All rights reserved. No part of this publication may be reproduced, stored or transmitted in any form or by any means, electronic, mechanical, photocopying, recording, scanning, or otherwise without written permission from the publisher. It is illegal to copy this book, post it to a website, or distribute it by any other means without permission.

First edition

This book was professionally typeset on Reedsy.
Find out more at reedsy.com

Contents

1 Chapter 1: The Essence of Leadership — 1
2 Chapter 2: Communicating with Impact — 3
3 Chapter 3: Building Trust Through Transparency — 5
4 Chapter 4: The Power of Active Listening — 7
5 Chapter 5: Crafting Your Leadership Brand — 9
6 Chapter 6: The Art of Persuasion — 11
7 Chapter 7: Navigating Conflict with Grace — 13
8 Chapter 8: Leading by Example — 15
9 Chapter 9: Emotional Intelligence in Leadership — 16
10 Chapter 10: The Role of Feedback — 18
11 Chapter 11: Building Inclusive Relationships — 20
12 Chapter 12: Public Speaking Pitfalls to Avoid — 22
13 Chapter 13: Storytelling in Public Speaking — 24
14 Chapter 14: The Dynamics of Body Language — 26
15 Chapter 15: Handling Stage Fright — 28
16 Chapter 16: Networking and Relationship Building — 30
17 Chapter 17: Continuous Improvement and Lifelong Learning — 32

1

Chapter 1: The Essence of Leadership

Leadership isn't merely about holding a title or occupying a position of authority. It is about the ability to influence, inspire, and drive others toward a common goal. At its core, leadership embodies vision, commitment, and a profound understanding of human nature. Effective leaders recognize that their actions set the tone for their teams and that every decision they make impacts not just the immediate outcomes but the broader organizational culture.

True leadership is deeply rooted in authenticity and integrity. Authentic leaders lead with their values, making decisions that reflect their principles. They are transparent about their motives and consistent in their actions, which builds trust among their followers. Integrity, on the other hand, involves doing the right thing even when no one is watching. Leaders with integrity create an environment of trust and respect, where team members feel safe to express their ideas and take risks.

Another vital aspect of leadership is emotional intelligence. Leaders who are emotionally intelligent are aware of their own emotions and can manage them effectively. They also understand and empathize with the emotions of others, which enables them to build strong relationships and manage conflicts constructively. Emotional intelligence in leadership fosters a supportive and collaborative team environment, where individuals feel valued and motivated to contribute their best.

Lastly, effective leadership involves a continuous journey of self-improvement and learning. Great leaders are not born; they are made through experience, reflection, and a commitment to personal growth. They seek feedback, learn from their mistakes, and are always looking for ways to improve their skills and knowledge. By embracing a mindset of lifelong learning, leaders can adapt to changing circumstances and continue to lead effectively in any situation.

2

Chapter 2: Communicating with Impact

Public speaking is much more than delivering words to an audience; it is about creating a connection and leaving a lasting impact. A powerful speech can inspire, motivate, and drive change. To achieve this, speakers must craft their messages with clarity, purpose, and emotion. Every speech should have a clear objective and be tailored to the audience's needs and interests.

The foundation of impactful communication lies in storytelling. Humans are naturally drawn to stories, and a well-crafted narrative can make a message more relatable and memorable. Effective speakers use stories to illustrate their points, evoke emotions, and create a vivid picture in the minds of their audience. By weaving personal anecdotes, case studies, and vivid imagery into their speeches, speakers can make their messages resonate more deeply.

Another key element of public speaking is non-verbal communication. Body language, facial expressions, and vocal tone play a crucial role in how a message is received. Confident and open body language, such as maintaining eye contact, using expressive gestures, and adopting a strong posture, can reinforce the speaker's words and convey confidence and credibility. Similarly, varying vocal tone and pace can keep the audience engaged and highlight important points.

Preparation and practice are essential for effective public speaking. Great speakers invest time in crafting their messages, rehearsing their delivery, and anticipating potential questions or challenges. They also seek feedback from others to refine their performance. By practicing regularly and learning from each experience, speakers can build confidence and improve their skills over time.

3

Chapter 3: Building Trust Through Transparency

Trust is the cornerstone of any successful relationship, whether personal or professional. Building and maintaining trust requires transparency, honesty, and consistency. When leaders are transparent in their actions and decisions, they create an environment of openness and trust. Transparency involves sharing information openly, being honest about challenges and mistakes, and demonstrating accountability.

Honesty is fundamental to building trust. Leaders who are honest in their communication and actions earn the respect and loyalty of their followers. This means being truthful even when the news is not positive and avoiding half-truths or omissions. When leaders are honest, they create a culture where team members feel comfortable sharing their own ideas and concerns, leading to better collaboration and problem-solving.

Consistency is another critical factor in building trust. Consistent actions and decisions signal reliability and predictability, which helps to build confidence and trust. Leaders who are consistent in their values, behavior, and expectations create a stable and supportive environment where team members know what to expect and feel secure in their roles.

Building trust also involves actively seeking and valuing the input of others. Leaders who listen to their team members, involve them in decision-making, and show appreciation for their contributions foster a sense of trust and mutual respect. By creating a culture of transparency and inclusivity, leaders can build strong, trusting relationships that drive team success.

4

Chapter 4: The Power of Active Listening

Listening is a crucial yet often overlooked skill in leadership and communication. Active listening goes beyond hearing words; it involves fully engaging with the speaker, understanding their message, and responding thoughtfully. Leaders who practice active listening create a supportive and collaborative environment where team members feel heard and valued.

Active listening involves several key techniques. First, it requires giving the speaker your full attention. This means putting aside distractions, making eye contact, and showing genuine interest in what they are saying. It also involves acknowledging the speaker's message through nodding, paraphrasing, or summarizing their points to show understanding.

Empathy is another critical component of active listening. Empathetic listeners try to understand the speaker's feelings and perspectives, which helps to build rapport and trust. By showing empathy, leaders can create a safe space for open and honest communication, where team members feel comfortable sharing their thoughts and concerns.

Responding thoughtfully is the final step in active listening. This involves asking questions for clarification, providing feedback, and offering support or solutions as needed. Thoughtful responses demonstrate that the leader values the speaker's input and is committed to addressing their needs and concerns.

By mastering the art of active listening, leaders can enhance their communication skills, build stronger relationships, and create a more inclusive and collaborative team environment.

5

Chapter 5: Crafting Your Leadership Brand

Every leader has a unique style and presence that forms their leadership brand. This brand is a reflection of your values, strengths, and the way you interact with others. To develop a cohesive and authentic leadership brand, you must first understand your strengths and areas for improvement. Self-awareness is the cornerstone of personal branding.

Begin by identifying the qualities that define your leadership style. Are you a visionary who inspires others with big ideas, or a hands-on leader who excels at executing plans? Understanding your natural tendencies and how they align with your leadership goals will help you craft a brand that feels genuine and powerful.

Next, focus on consistency. Your leadership brand should be evident in every aspect of your professional life, from the way you communicate to the decisions you make. Consistency builds trust and credibility, as people come to know what to expect from you. Align your actions, words, and behaviors with the values that define your brand, and be mindful of how you are perceived by others.

Finally, invest in continuous development. The most effective leaders are those who are committed to growth and improvement. Seek feedback from peers and mentors, and be open to learning from your experiences. By constantly refining your skills and expanding your knowledge, you can ensure that your leadership brand remains relevant and impactful.

6

Chapter 6: The Art of Persuasion

Persuasion is a powerful tool in leadership and public speaking. It involves influencing others while respecting their viewpoints and encouraging collaboration. The art of persuasion is built on three key pillars: ethos, pathos, and logos.

Ethos refers to the credibility of the speaker. To persuade others, you must establish yourself as a trustworthy and knowledgeable authority on the subject. This can be achieved through demonstrating expertise, sharing relevant experiences, and maintaining a reputation for integrity.

Pathos involves appealing to the emotions of your audience. Emotional appeals can make your message more relatable and memorable. Use stories, anecdotes, and vivid imagery to evoke emotions such as empathy, hope, or urgency. By connecting with your audience on an emotional level, you can create a deeper impact and motivate them to take action.

Logos is the logical aspect of persuasion. This involves presenting clear, well-reasoned arguments supported by evidence and data. Use facts, statistics, and logical reasoning to build a compelling case for your message. A strong logical foundation, combined with emotional appeal and credibility, will make your persuasive efforts more effective.

Mastering the art of persuasion requires practice and a deep understanding of your audience. Tailor your approach to their needs, preferences, and values. By combining ethos, pathos, and logos, you can influence others in a respectful and impactful way.

7

Chapter 7: Navigating Conflict with Grace

Conflict is inevitable in any relationship, but how you handle it defines your leadership. Constructive conflict management can turn disagreements into opportunities for growth and understanding. To navigate conflict with grace, focus on communication, empathy, and problem-solving.

Effective communication is essential for resolving conflicts. Be clear and direct in expressing your concerns, and listen actively to the perspectives of others. Avoid blame or accusations, and focus on discussing the issues at hand. By fostering open and honest communication, you can create an environment where conflicts are addressed constructively.

Empathy plays a crucial role in conflict resolution. Try to understand the emotions and viewpoints of those involved in the conflict. Show empathy by acknowledging their feelings and validating their experiences. This helps to build trust and rapport, making it easier to find common ground.

Problem-solving is the final step in navigating conflict. Collaborate with those involved to identify potential solutions and agree on a course of action. Be open to compromise and seek win-win outcomes that address the needs of all parties. By focusing on problem-solving rather than winning, you can resolve conflicts in a way that strengthens relationships and fosters collaboration.

8

Chapter 8: Leading by Example

Actions speak louder than words, especially in leadership. Leading by example means embodying the values and behaviors you wish to see in others. This approach to leadership is rooted in integrity, consistency, and accountability.

Integrity involves aligning your actions with your values and principles. When you lead with integrity, you demonstrate honesty, fairness, and ethical behavior in all your interactions. This sets a positive example for others and creates a culture of trust and respect.

Consistency is key to leading by example. Your actions should consistently reflect your values and leadership brand. This means being reliable, dependable, and predictable in your behavior. Consistency builds credibility and confidence, as others know they can rely on you to act with integrity and purpose.

Accountability is another essential aspect of leading by example. Take responsibility for your actions and decisions, and be transparent about your successes and failures. By holding yourself accountable, you encourage others to do the same and create an environment of mutual trust and respect.

Leading by example inspires and motivates others to follow your lead. When you consistently demonstrate the values and behaviors you wish to see in your team, you create a positive and supportive culture that drives success and collaboration.

9

Chapter 9: Emotional Intelligence in Leadership

Emotional intelligence (EI) is the ability to recognize, understand, and manage our own emotions and those of others. Leaders with high EI are better equipped to handle interpersonal relationships judiciously and empathetically. This chapter delves into the components of emotional intelligence and how they contribute to effective leadership.

The first component of EI is self-awareness. This involves understanding your own emotions, strengths, weaknesses, and triggers. Self-aware leaders can recognize how their emotions affect their thoughts and behavior, which allows them to make more informed and rational decisions. By being aware of their emotional state, leaders can also better manage their stress and maintain a positive outlook.

Self-regulation is another crucial aspect of EI. This refers to the ability to control impulsive behaviors and emotions, and to think before acting. Leaders who can self-regulate are able to stay calm under pressure, adapt to changing circumstances, and maintain their composure in challenging situations. Self-regulation also involves being open to change and embracing new ideas.

Empathy is the ability to understand and share the feelings of others. Empathetic leaders can connect with their team members on a deeper level, showing genuine concern for their well-being. This fosters a supportive and inclusive environment where team members feel valued and understood. Empathy also enhances communication, as leaders can better interpret non-verbal cues and respond appropriately.

The final component of EI is social skills. This includes effective communication, conflict resolution, and relationship-building. Leaders with strong social skills can build rapport with team members, navigate social complexities, and lead by example. They are adept at managing conflicts, motivating others, and fostering a collaborative team environment.

By cultivating emotional intelligence, leaders can enhance their ability to connect with others, build trust, and lead effectively in any situation.

10

Chapter 10: The Role of Feedback

Constructive feedback is an essential tool for personal and professional growth. It helps individuals understand their strengths and areas for improvement, and provides guidance on how to enhance their performance. This chapter explores the importance of feedback and how to give and receive it effectively.

Giving feedback requires clarity, specificity, and empathy. Effective feedback should be specific and focused on behaviors, not personal attributes. For example, instead of saying "You are disorganized," a more constructive approach would be "I noticed that the reports were submitted late. Let's discuss ways to improve time management." This focuses on the behavior that needs improvement and provides a starting point for a constructive conversation.

Empathy is crucial when giving feedback. Consider the recipient's perspective and emotions, and deliver feedback in a way that is supportive and encouraging. Use positive language and highlight the recipient's strengths while addressing areas for improvement. This helps to maintain their self-esteem and motivation.

Receiving feedback is equally important. Approach feedback with an open mind and a willingness to learn. Listen actively, ask for clarification if needed, and reflect on the feedback received. Even if the feedback is challenging, view it as an opportunity for growth and improvement. By embracing feedback, you can continuously enhance your skills and performance.

Creating a feedback culture within a team or organization fosters continuous improvement and open communication. Encourage team members to give and receive feedback regularly, and lead by example by actively seeking and acting on feedback. This creates an environment where everyone feels valued and supported in their development.

11

Chapter 11: Building Inclusive Relationships

Inclusivity is key to fostering trust and collaboration in diverse teams. Building inclusive relationships involves recognizing and valuing different perspectives, creating an environment where everyone feels respected and valued. This chapter explores strategies for promoting inclusivity in leadership and communication.

Inclusive leaders recognize the importance of diversity and actively seek to include diverse voices in decision-making. They understand that diverse teams bring a wide range of experiences, ideas, and perspectives that can enhance creativity and innovation. By valuing diversity, leaders create a culture where everyone feels heard and valued.

Creating an inclusive environment involves promoting mutual respect and understanding. Encourage open dialogue and actively listen to the perspectives of others. Show empathy and validate the experiences and feelings of team members. This helps to build trust and rapport, and fosters a sense of belonging.

Inclusivity also involves being aware of and addressing unconscious biases. Reflect on your own biases and take steps to mitigate their impact. Promote fairness and equity in decision-making, and ensure that all team members have equal opportunities for growth and development.

CHAPTER 11: BUILDING INCLUSIVE RELATIONSHIPS

By building inclusive relationships, leaders can create a supportive and collaborative team environment where everyone feels valued and motivated to contribute their best.

12

Chapter 12: Public Speaking Pitfalls to Avoid

Even seasoned speakers can fall into common traps that undermine their effectiveness. This chapter highlights the most frequent mistakes in public speaking and provides tips on how to avoid them.

One common pitfall is overloading slides with text or data. Visual aids should enhance your message, not overwhelm it. Use slides to highlight key points, and keep text concise and easy to read. Avoid reading directly from the slides, as this can disengage your audience. Instead, use them as a visual complement to your spoken words.

Neglecting the audience's needs is another common mistake. Effective speakers tailor their message to the interests and preferences of their audience. Research your audience beforehand and consider what they care about. Use language and examples that resonate with them, and engage them with questions or interactive elements.

Another pitfall is failing to practice. Even the most well-prepared speech can fall flat if not delivered confidently. Practice your speech multiple times, focusing on your delivery, pacing, and body language. Seek feedback from others and make adjustments as needed. Practicing regularly builds confidence and ensures a smoother delivery.

Finally, avoid speaking in a monotone or using filler words excessively.

CHAPTER 12: PUBLIC SPEAKING PITFALLS TO AVOID

Vary your vocal tone and pace to keep your audience engaged. Use pauses effectively to emphasize key points and give your audience time to absorb the information. Be mindful of filler words such as "um" and "uh," and practice speaking clearly and confidently.

By being aware of these common pitfalls and taking steps to avoid them, you can enhance your public speaking skills and deliver more impactful and engaging presentations.

13

Chapter 13: Storytelling in Public Speaking

Stories are a powerful way to connect with your audience and make your message memorable. This chapter will delve into the art of storytelling in public speaking, offering techniques to craft and deliver compelling narratives.

To begin with, a good story has a clear structure: a beginning, middle, and end. The beginning sets the scene and introduces the characters and context. The middle presents the conflict or challenge, creating tension and engagement. The end provides resolution and reinforces the key message. By following this structure, you can create a coherent and engaging narrative that captures your audience's attention.

Vivid imagery and sensory details are crucial in storytelling. Use descriptive language to paint a picture in the minds of your audience, making the story come to life. Include details that appeal to the senses, such as sights, sounds, and emotions. This helps to immerse the audience in the story and makes the message more impactful.

Emotion is a key element of effective storytelling. Stories that evoke emotions such as joy, sadness, or excitement resonate more deeply with the audience. Share personal anecdotes or real-life examples that illustrate your points and evoke empathy. By connecting with your audience on an emotional level, you can make your message more relatable and memorable.

Lastly, practice is essential for delivering a compelling story. Rehearse your story multiple times, focusing on your delivery, pacing, and body language. Pay attention to how you use pauses, tone, and gestures to enhance the narrative. With practice, you can refine your storytelling skills and create a more powerful impact.

14

Chapter 14: The Dynamics of Body Language

Non-verbal communication plays a significant role in how your message is received. This chapter explores the dynamics of body language and how to use it effectively in public speaking and leadership.

Body language encompasses gestures, facial expressions, posture, and eye contact. Each of these elements can reinforce or undermine your spoken words. For example, open and expansive gestures convey confidence and openness, while closed or defensive gestures may signal discomfort or insecurity.

Facial expressions are a powerful tool for conveying emotions. A genuine smile can create a positive and welcoming atmosphere, while a furrowed brow may indicate concern or seriousness. Be mindful of your facial expressions and ensure they align with the emotions you want to convey.

Posture is another important aspect of body language. A strong and upright posture conveys confidence and authority, while slouching or fidgeting can detract from your message. Stand tall, keep your shoulders back, and avoid crossing your arms. This creates an impression of confidence and approachability.

Eye contact is crucial for building rapport and trust with your audience.

Maintain eye contact with different members of the audience to create a sense of connection and engagement. Avoid looking down or constantly shifting your gaze, as this can make you appear unsure or distracted.

By mastering the dynamics of body language, you can enhance your communication skills and create a more impactful and engaging presence.

15

Chapter 15: Handling Stage Fright

Stage fright is a common challenge for many speakers. This chapter provides techniques for overcoming anxiety and building confidence when speaking in public.

First, it's important to recognize that stage fright is a natural response to the stress of public speaking. Even experienced speakers can feel nervous before a presentation. The key is to manage this anxiety and use it to your advantage.

Preparation is essential for building confidence. Thoroughly prepare your speech, practice multiple times, and familiarize yourself with the venue and audience. The more prepared you are, the more confident you will feel.

Visualization is a powerful technique for overcoming stage fright. Before your presentation, visualize yourself speaking confidently and successfully. Imagine the positive reactions of the audience and the successful delivery of your message. This helps to create a positive mindset and reduce anxiety.

Breathing exercises can also help to calm nerves and reduce anxiety. Practice deep breathing before and during your presentation to stay relaxed and focused. Slow, deep breaths can help to steady your voice and calm your nerves.

Finally, focus on the message, not yourself. Remember that the purpose of your speech is to share valuable information and connect with your audience. Shift your focus from your own anxiety to the impact you want to have on your audience. This can help to reduce self-consciousness and build confidence.

16

Chapter 16: Networking and Relationship Building

Leadership and public speaking often involve networking and building relationships. This chapter offers strategies for effective networking and building meaningful connections.

Networking is about creating and nurturing professional relationships. Start by identifying your networking goals and the type of connections you want to make. Attend events, join professional organizations, and engage in online communities to meet like-minded individuals.

When networking, focus on building genuine relationships rather than collecting contacts. Show genuine interest in others, listen actively, and ask thoughtful questions. This helps to build rapport and establish a foundation of trust.

Follow up with your connections after networking events. Send a personalized message expressing your appreciation for the conversation and suggesting ways to stay in touch. This demonstrates your commitment to building a meaningful relationship.

Nurture your relationships over time by staying in touch and offering support. Share relevant information, provide assistance when needed, and celebrate the successes of your connections. By investing in your relationships, you can create a strong network of support and collaboration.

CHAPTER 16: NETWORKING AND RELATIONSHIP BUILDING

Networking is a valuable skill that can enhance your leadership and public speaking success. By building and nurturing meaningful relationships, you can expand your opportunities and achieve your goals.

17

Chapter 17: Continuous Improvement and Lifelong Learning

The journey of leadership and public speaking is one of continuous improvement and lifelong learning. This chapter emphasizes the importance of staying curious, seeking new knowledge, and continuously refining your skills to stay relevant and effective.

Continuous improvement involves regularly assessing your strengths and areas for growth. Seek feedback from peers, mentors, and team members to identify opportunities for development. Set clear goals and create a plan to achieve them, incorporating regular practice and reflection into your routine. By embracing a mindset of continuous improvement, you can enhance your leadership and communication skills over time.

Lifelong learning is about maintaining a curiosity and openness to new ideas. Stay informed about the latest trends and research in leadership, public speaking, and your industry. Attend workshops, conferences, and training sessions to expand your knowledge and network with other professionals. Read books, articles, and listen to podcasts to gain new insights and perspectives. Lifelong learning keeps you adaptable and resilient in the face of change.

Finally, share your knowledge and experiences with others. Mentoring, coaching, and teaching can reinforce your own learning and help others grow.

CHAPTER 17: CONTINUOUS IMPROVEMENT AND LIFELONG LEARNING

By giving back to your community, you can create a positive impact and contribute to the development of future leaders.

Book Description

Action Speaks Louder: Leadership, Public Speaking, and the Art of Building Trust in Relationships

In a world where actions truly speak louder than words, effective leadership and communication are paramount. "Action Speaks Louder" is your essential guide to mastering the art of leadership, public speaking, and building trust in relationships. Drawing on timeless principles and modern strategies, this book offers practical insights and actionable advice to help you become a more influential and inspiring leader.

Discover the core traits that define effective leadership, and learn how to lead by example with authenticity and integrity. Uncover the secrets of impactful communication, from crafting compelling narratives to mastering the nuances of body language and vocal tone. Explore the power of transparency, empathy, and active listening in building trust and fostering strong relationships.

Each chapter is packed with real-world examples, practical techniques, and thought-provoking insights to help you navigate the complexities of leadership and communication. Whether you're a seasoned leader looking to refine your skills or an aspiring speaker seeking to make your mark, "Action Speaks Louder" provides the tools and inspiration you need to achieve your goals.

Embrace the journey of continuous improvement and lifelong learning, and transform your leadership and public speaking capabilities. With "Action Speaks Louder," you'll gain the confidence and competence to lead with impact, speak with authority, and build lasting trust in every relationship.

www.ingramcontent.com/pod-product-compliance
Lightning Source LLC
LaVergne TN
LVHW020500080526
838202LV00057B/6065